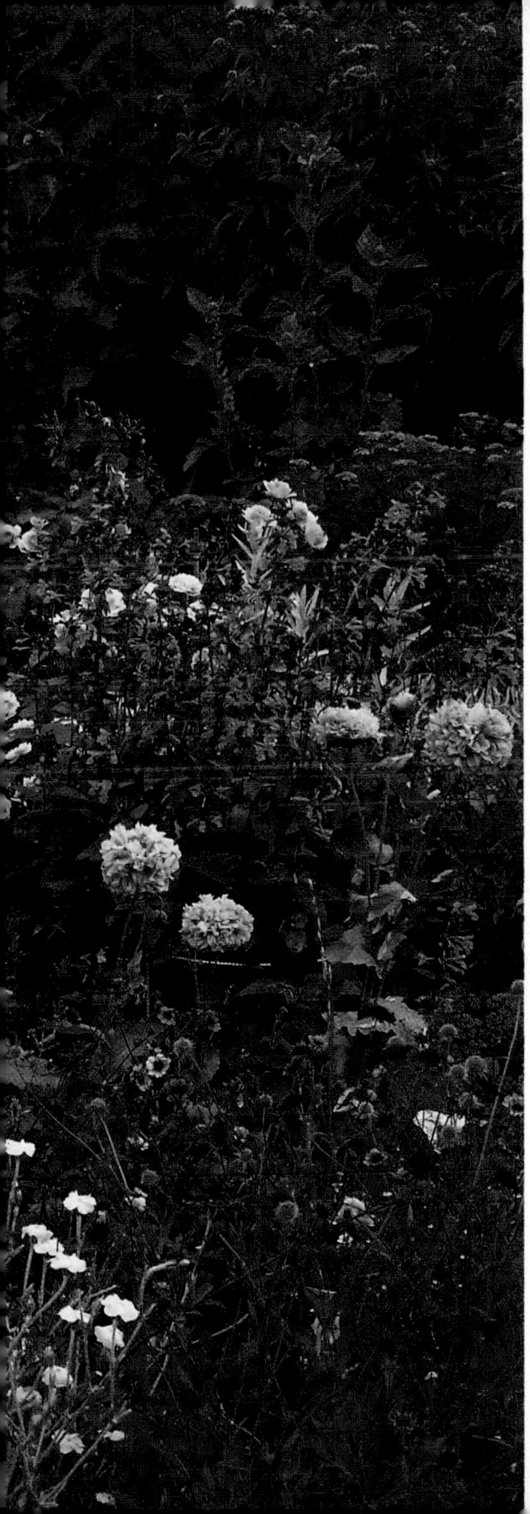

Success with

Herbaceous Borders

DOROTHÉE WAECHTER

Series Editor:
LESLEY YOUNG

Introduction

A wealth of flowering plants

Herbaceous plants are an endless joy in any garden. Their variety is so great that they work their colourful magic throughout the entire flowering season in every corner of the garden, whether sunny or shady, against a house wall or in the middle of a lawn.
In this guide, garden expert Dorothée Waechter explains how to make the most of the huge range of plants on offer to create a quite splendid herbaceous garden. Whether you have decided on island beds or borders, mixed beds of colourful plants or plants in different shades of one colour, the author provides plenty of ideas for several lovely designs. There is advice on how to employ colour to your best advantage and how to combine different colours effectively. There are also tips on the use of scented herbaceous plants and on plantings in large containers and pots. In addition, the text contains all the basic information you will need to know about where to place different species of plants, their shapes of growth and flowering times, plus detailed instructions on how to plant herbaceous plants and how to care for them properly throughout the year.

Contents

Island beds can break up larger areas of lawn.

Columbine

... and iris.

The author
Dorothée Waechter is a garden designer who specializes in herbaceous plants. She contributes frequent articles on plants and gardens to numerous newspapers and periodicals and is the author of a number of gardening books.

The photographers
Jürgen Becker studied fine art and film-making. For the last fourteen years he has supplied photographs to well-known calendar, book and magazine publishers.
Marlon Nickig became known for her unusual garden and flower photographs in FAZ magazine. She also works for several well-known book and magazine publishers.
Plant and garden photographs are among the best-known subjects of both photographers.

The illustrator
Elfie Vierck-Petschelt studied at the Muthesius-Werkkunstschule in Kiel under Professor Heinrich Arpe. She now works as an illustrator for several well-known publishing houses, magazines and for Bavarian Television. Her usual subjects are plants and animals.

NB: Please read the Author's Notes on page 61 so that your enjoyment of herbaceous plants may not be spoiled.

All about herbaceous plants

A multitude of plants

With flowers of blue, lilac, red, yellow or white, herbaceous plants form an attractive, eye-catching feature in any garden. The following pages will supply you with all the necessary basic information you need to know concerning the preferred position, shapes of growth and flowering times of herbaceous plants for you to be able to plan your own beautiful flowering beds.

Left: In late spring oriental poppy (Papaver orientale "Catharina") transforms this bed into a sea of flowers.
Top: An attractive variety of delphinium (Delphinium "Spindrift").

A multitude of plants

What are herbaceous plants?

Herbaceous plants are perennial plants that, in contrast to plants that form woody stems and branches, such as trees or shrubs, have soft stalks and leaves. Those parts of the plant that are above ground usually wither during the winter. All herbaceous plants produce new shoots every year in the spring. The buds from which this new growth will shoot lie close to, or below, the soil. Herbaceous plants can be divided into groups according to different criteria.
Bedding herbaceous plants grow in most garden soils and hardly require any special care, which is one reason why they are so suitable for novice gardeners to grow.
Large, ornamental herbaceous plants are a sub-group of bedding herbaceous plants. They have large, conspicuous flowers and there is a large range of varieties within each species.
Wintergreen herbaceous plants retain their foliage throughout the winter. The old foliage does not die until the beginning of the spring when new shoots begin to grow again. One example is barrenwort (*Epimedium*).
Evergreen herbaceous plants, like periwinkle (*Vinca minor*), constantly renew their leaves independently of the rhythm of the seasons. Their leaves do not, therefore, dry up in the winter.
Sub-shrubs are often included among the herbaceous plants even though their stalks do become woody. The branches will survive mild winters. Should the branches freeze and die, the plant will produce new shoots from the rootstock. One example of this type of plant is lavender (*Lavandula*).
Bulbous and tuberous plants are counted among herbaceous plants botanically but require different treatment and care on account of their bulbs or tubers. They are, therefore, considered to belong to a different group in the gardening world. Examples include crocus (*Crocus*) and tulips (*Tulipa*).

Where do herbaceous plants come from?

Herbaceous plants originate from the temperate climatic zones of the northern and southern hemispheres, between the tropical and polar regions. In these regions, herbaceous plants have adapted to temperature changes through four distinct seasons. The herbaceous plants from alpine and Mediterranean areas are grouped separately from other herbaceous plants.
Alpine herbaceous plants originate from mountainous regions. Examples include houseleek (*Sempervivum*), saxifrage (*Saxifraga*) and low-growing campanula (*Campanula*).
Mediterranean herbaceous plants are at home in the regions around the Mediterranean Sea. Among these are lavender (*Lavandula angustifolia*), red valerian (*Centranthus ruber*) and Cupid's dart (*Catanche caerulea*).
NB: Alpine and Mediterranean herbaceous plants will definitely require winter protection in the garden (see p. 52).

How were the herbaceous plants named?

The common names of plants often vary from region to region but their Latin names are valid internationally. The Latin name consists of the genus name followed by the species name. A variety name, usually given in inverted commas, may supplement the species name, for example, *Papaver orientale* "Catharina" (see photograph, pp. 4/5).
The genus: Closely related herbaceous plant species are grouped together under the genus name.
The species: Herbaceous plants from one species can be crossed with each other but not with herbaceous plants of another species.
Among herbaceous plants of the same species, certain features, like the colour of the flowers, may be different and these factors can be used to develop different varieties.

Herbaceous plants look good even in formal gardens.

The variety: Members of the same species of herbaceous plants that all have the same characteristics form one variety. Most varieties will only retain their characteristics when propagated through division, as this is the only way that their genetic material will remain unchanged. When seeds are formed, however, the genetic material is mixed. In order to retain a variety, you will have to prevent the plant from forming seed.

Raising new herbaceous plants

The intensive raising of plants these days means that the wide range of herbaceous plants on offer is steadily increasing. Among the most important goals are pure, new flower colours and shapes, compact growth characteristics, long flowering times and lowered susceptibility to infestation by pests and diseases.

The testing of new varieties: The characteristics and qualities of new herbaceous plant varieties are tested in specialist nurseries before the new variety is put on the market.

Leucanthemum maximum.

Flower shapes

It is the flowers of herbaceous plants that draw the eye initially. Both the range of colours and the many different shapes of the flowers and flowerheads are fascinating. Many herbaceous plants, like marsh marigold (*Trollius*), have large, individual flowerheads. Many have bell-shaped flowers like those of *Platycodon* (see p. 15) or the more open, bowl shape of the poppy (*Papaver*).
More unusual are the flower shapes of columbine (*Aquilegia*) and iris (*Iris*).

Delphiniums in many shades of blue.

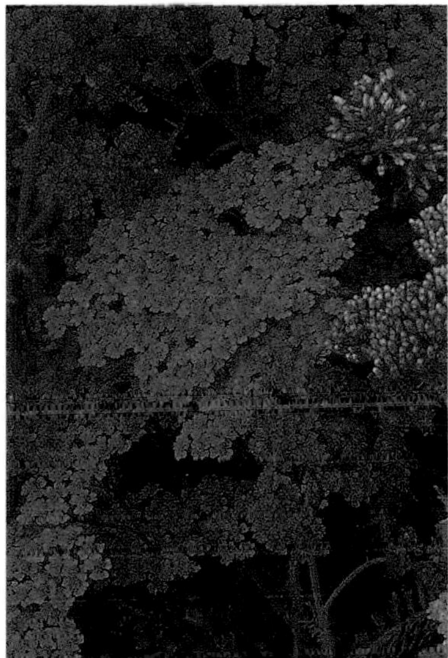

Achillea "Terracotta".

Papaver orientale "Alibaba".

Aquilegia caerulea hybrid.

Iris barbata hybrid.

Trollius europaeus.

In many herbaceous plants the individual flowers are grouped together in flowerheads. Typical shapes are those of the candle-shaped racemes of Delphinium and the umbel flowerheads of yarrow (Achillea). The branching panicles produced by astilbe (Astilbe) (see p. 15) are a common feature of herbaceous plants. The "daisy" shape of the many flowers of Leucanthemum is also found quite often. As with all compositae, the mass of tiny flowers gives the impression of being one single large flower.

Botany

1 Groundcover plants *will quickly fill large areas with their long shoots and underground rhizomes.*

The typical impression of a herbaceous plant is of one with many upright-growing, individual shoots.

Shapes of growth

The shape of growth of a herbaceous plant is derived from the size and arrangement of the leaves and flowers and the direction of growth of the shoots.

Cushion plants (illustration 3) are low-growing at heights between 5 and 30 cm (2-12 in). The shoots and foliage form small, flat-growing or slightly domed cushions. Cushion-forming plants are suitable for edging a herbaceous border, for rockeries and for the edges of paths.

Ground-cover herbaceous plants (illustration 1) grow like cushion-forming herbaceous plants but form longer shoots or underground rhizomes. They can attain heights of 5-40 cm (2-16 in) and will produce a dense carpet over larger areas. They are suitable for planting on a slope under woody plants.

Rosettes (illustration 2) are plants with a circular arrangement of leaves that lie like scales beneath each other. They attain heights of 5-25 cm (2-10 in). Smaller rosettes do well at the front of a herbaceous border. Large rosettes will also look good in the background.

Bushy clumps produce many shoots growing close to each other, to a height of 25 cm (10 in) or more. The species characteristics and habit of growth of the underground parts of a bushy clump also influence its shape of growth above ground. For example, the autumn-flowering asters (*Aster novi belgii, A. novae-angliae*) have short, lateral underground shoots (illustration 6). Increasing depletion of light and nutrients among the central shoots leads to a bare centre to the clump after a few years. Two sub-groups can be distinguished among plants that form clumps or clusters.

● The shoots of upright-growing clumps (illustration 4) form an

2 Rosette *plants have leaves arranged in a circular, scale-like formation. One plant may consist of several rosettes.*

3 Cushion plants *form small cushions with their shoots and leaves. The flowers appear above the tangled growth.*

4 ***Upright clumps*** *have many shoots.*

5 ***Overhanging*** *clumps droop.*

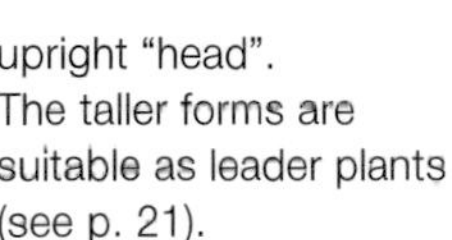

upright "head".
The taller forms are suitable as leader plants (see p. 21).

- Clumps that grow in a downward-curving fashion (illustration 5) open up outwards in a fan-like shape. They are ideal for linking plant groups with each other.

Sub-shrubs do not have a typical shape of growth. Most of them attain a height of up to 60 cm (24 in). Taller sub-shrubs are conspicuous all year round in a bed and should, therefore, complement the leader plants in the bed.

Life expectancy

How long a herbaceous plant will live in a garden will depend on:

- whether the conditions in the position in which it is planted suit its requirements (see pp. 16 and 17);
- the health of the individual plant;
- the capacity of the plant for growing vigorously;
- the species of the individual plant.

With the right care, most species of herbaceous plant will thrive in a suitable position for eight to 20 years. You can extend this time through rejuvenation (see p. 52). Other species are either very shortlived or even longer lived.

Short lifespan: Short-lived herbaceous plants generally live for only four years. Allow the flowerheads to ripen into seedheads which can sow themselves. The seedlings will look slightly different to the parent plants (see p. 6), but the differences are not very noticeable.

Short-lived herbaceous plants include columbine (*Aquilegia*) and flax (*Linum*).

Long-living plants: Herbaceous plants with a long lifespan may live for up to 60 years. During the first few years they grow slowly and will hardly flower at all. Among these plants are day lilies (*Hemerocallis*) and peony (*Paeonia*).

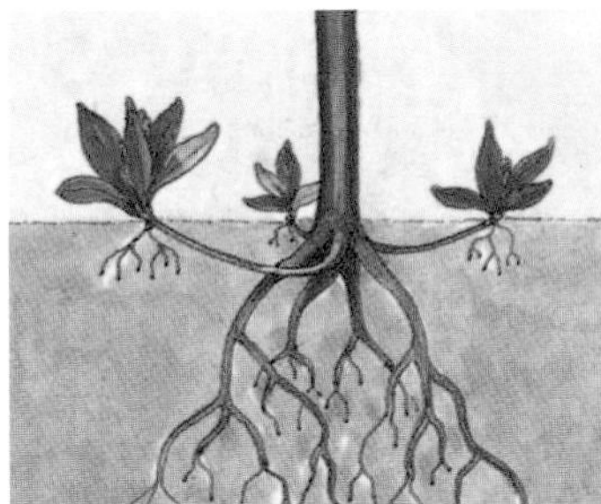

6 ***Autumn asters*** *form underground rhizomes which help the clumps to spread outwards.*

Crane's bill is a beautiful groundcover plant for semi-shady edges of shrubberies and stands of trees.

Position

Herbaceous plants have varying requirements with respect to factors such as light, temperature, soil consistency and soil humidity (see pp. 16 and 17).
These requirements determine whether a plant will thrive in a certain position or whether it will fail. For this reason, you will need to check the conditions in your garden and then choose suitable herbaceous plants.
Light: This is a most important ingredient. Herbaceous plants that are adapted to sunny positions will not grow well in shade and vice versa.
Observe a particular position on sunny days to determine whether it is mostly sunny or shady and for how long and when the sun shines directly on to the bed.

- Sunny positions will be in full sunlight most of the time during the day, particularly during the midday hours.
- Semi-shady beds will receive sunlight only temporarily – for example, in the morning or evening. Alternatively, a loose canopy of leaves may allow a few rays of sunshine through all day long.

● Shady positions do not receive any direct sunlight. The conditions closely resemble those of a woodland setting.
Temperature: Most herbaceous plants can tolerate the normal conditions of a temperate climate. Frost-sensitive and warmth-loving plants will, however, require special treatment (see below).
Soil consistency: Most bedding herbaceous plants will thrive on normal garden soils. You can find out how to test your soil and also improve it on page 18.
Soil humidity: Nearly all herbaceous plants prefer a consistently moist soil in which water can drain away easily (see p. 18).
My tip: Detailed information on the requirements of individual species and varieties can be obtained from garden centres or from the labels attached to the plants when you buy them. The plant catalogues of specialist nurseries should also be a good source of information.

Climate

Frost-sensitive herbaceous plants will definitely require winter protection (see p. 52). Most alpine and Mediterranean plants are included in this group (see p. 6). Other examples include *Kniphofia*, autumn anemone (*Anemone*) and *Ceratostigma*.
Warmth-loving herbaceous plants require a fully sunny position sheltered from the wind. Many of these species react sensitively to wet soils. The silver-grey-leafed herbaceous plants, plus *Aster amellus*, iris (*Iris barbata* hybrids), poppy (*Papaver orientale*) and scabious (*Scabiosa*) all belong among the warmth-loving herbaceous plants.

Types of garden environment

Herbaceous plants can be grown successfully in many different garden settings depending on the requirements of the individual species and varieties in question. The most likely settings in an average garden are beds, as a border to a shrubbery or stand of trees, in a rockery or along the bank of a pond or stream.
Beds: Nearly all bedding plants thrive in a flowerbed provided that their requirements in regard to soil and light conditions are met (see pp. 16 and 17). If it does not suit the requirements of the herbaceous plant, you can still improve the soil (see p. 18). The most important factor is whether the bed is sunny, semi-shady or shady.
As a border to shrubs or trees: This includes positions bordering hedges and the area underneath a spreading tree.
These sites are usually semi-shady to shady. Only the terrain to the south of a hedge will be sunny, and then only if there are no overhanging branches. Herbaceous plants as a border to shrubs or trees have to compete with them for nutrients and water. Only certain herbaceous plants like deadnettle (*Lamium maculatum*), barrenwort (*Epimedium* species) and true wild species that originate from this sort of habitat (see p. 39) can survive here.
Rockery: This type of garden environment is usually artificially constructed and is characterized by a nutrient-poor soil (see p. 19). Popular herbaceous plants for rockeries are pinks (*Dianthus*), stonecrop (*Sedum*) and whitlow grass (*Draba*).
Banks along water: This type of environment occurs in gardens with ponds or streams. The determining criterion for this setting is consistently moist soil. Apart from marsh marigold (*Trollius*), astilbe and day lily (*Hemerocallis*), very few herbaceous plants like it. Artificially built ponds, however, usually have a dry bank as the liner or basin will not allow water to escape.

Heliopsis scabra.

Herbaceous plants for sunny and shady positions

During the course of millions of years of evolution, individual herbaceous plant species have adapted to sunny, semi-shady or shady positions. In sunny positions, sneezewort (*Helenium*), balloon flower (*Platycodon*) and red hot poker (*Kniphofia*) will show their full flowering splendour in the summer. The flowers of *Heliopsis* will decorate a herbaceous border long into the autumn.

Helenium hybrid "Sonnenbraut".

Kniphofia hybrid.

Aconitum x arendsii.

Platycodon grandiflorum.

Astilbe "Diamant".

Primula vulgaris.

Many herbaceous plants grow best in the shade. The primrose (Primula vulgaris) grows well under trees and bushes and will flower in the spring before foliage appears on the trees so that it can snatch a little sunlight during its flowering period. Astilbe and monkshood (Aconitum) also prefer the shade. In the summer, they will add strong shades of colour to the often darker shady area of the garden.

A multitude of plants

Herbaceous plants for sunny positions

Name	Flowering time Colour	Height in cm/in Shapes of growth	Soil	Plants per sq m (sq yd) Space between plants	Comments
Achillea filipendulina yarrow	MS-EA golden yellow	80-120 cm (32-48 in) U	tolerates dryness	5-7 50-70 cm (20-28 in)	remove deadheads
Aster, species and varieties Michaelmas daisy and others	EA-MA various	80-150 cm (32-60 in) U/OH	damp, nutrient- rich	3-5 70-90 cm (28-36 in)	divide when cluster becomes bare
Aubrieta hybrids aubrieta	MSP-LSP red, pink, blue	5-10 cm (2-4 in) C	permeable	20 30 cm (12 in)	cut back after flowering
Delphinium hybrids delphinium	ES-MS + EA blue, white lilac	50-200 cm (20-80 in) U	loose, humus, nutrient-rich	3 90 cm (36 in)	tie up early, may come again
Dendranthema indicum hybrids autumn chrysanthemums	EA-LA various	50-100 cm (20-40 in) U	dry, containing lime, nutrient-rich	7-9 40-50 cm (16-20 in)	avoid wet winter conditions, tie up
Gypsophila paniculata baby's breath	MS-LS white	80-100 cm (32-40 in) OH	containing a little lime	3 90 cm (36 in)	only replant while young
Helenium hybrids sneezewort	MS-EA yellow, red, brown	80-100 cm (32-40 in) U	humus, nutrient- rich	5 70 cm (28 in)	cut back in ES, divide after 6 years
Heliopsis hybrids	MSP-MS yellow	90-170 cm (36-68 in) OH	loose, nutrient- rich	5 70 cm (28 in)	remove dead parts: extends flowering time
Hemerocallis hybrids day lily	ES-EA various	40-120 cm (16-48 in) OH	prefers moist conditions	3-5 70-90 cm (28-36 in)	remove deadheads
Iris barbata hybrids iris	LSP-ES various	40-100 cm (16-40 in) U	dry in summer, loose	7 50 cm (20 in)	remove dead parts, optimal planting time LS
Kniphofia hybrids red hot poker	ES-EA yellow, orange	70-100 cm (28-40 in) U	permeable, containing humus, nutrient-rich	5 70 cm (28 in)	winter protection, do not cut back leaves
Leucanthemum maximum	ES-EA white	80-120 cm (32-48 in) OH/U	medium heavy, containing lime	7 50 cm (20 in)	remove dead parts, add compost in autumn
Lupinus polyphyllus hybrids lupin	LSP-ES + EA various	80-100 cm (32-40 in) OH/U	sandy, does not like lime	7 50 cm (20 in)	cutting back after flowering encourages second flowering
Monarda hybrids bergamot	ES-LS red, white, lilac	80-150 cm (32-60 in) U	medium moist, nutrient-rich	7 50 cm (20 in)	winter protection, susceptible to mildew
Nepeta faassenii catmint	LSP-EA lavender blue	30-50 cm (12-20 in) OH	dry to slightly damp	12 30 cm (12 in)	cut back after flowering
Oenothera tetragona evening primrose	LSP-EA brilliant yellow	50-80 cm (20-32 in) U	nutrient-rich, loose	12 30 cm (12 in)	remove wilted flowers
Paeonia lactiflora, varieties ☠ peony	LSP-ES red, pink, white	50-110 cm (20-44 in) OH	nutrient-rich, medium acidic	1-3 80-100 cm (32-40 in)	optimal planting time autumn, remove dead flowers
Papaver orientale, varieties oriental poppy	LSP-ES red, orange, white	60-110 cm (24-44 in) OH	permeable, nutrient-rich	1-3 80-100 cm (32-40 in)	avoid replanting, optimal planting time autumn
Phlox paniculatum, varieties garden phlox	ES-EA red, white, lilac	80-140 cm (32-56 in) U	damp, nutrient- rich, permeable	5 90 cm (36 in)	remove dead flowerheads
Rudbeckia fulgida coneflower	ES-EA golden yellow	60-80 cm (24-32 in) U	containing humus, nutrient-rich	9 40 cm (16 in)	rejuvenate after 5-6 years
Salvia nemorosa, varieties perennial sage	ES-MS lilac blue	50-60 cm (20-24 in) U	damp, nutrient- rich, containing lime	9 40 cm (16 in)	cutting back after flowering encourages second flowering

Herbaceous plants for semi-shady and shady positions

Name	Flowering time Colour	Height in cm/in Shapes of growth	Soil	Plants per sq m (sq yd) Space between plants	Comments
Aconitum species and varieties ☠ monkshood	ES-LS, EA-MA blue, light yellow	100-150 cm (40-60 in) U	damp to moist, cont. humus, nutrient-rich	7 50 cm (20 in)	cut back after flowering
Alchemilla mollis lady's mantle	ES greeny yellow	40 cm (16 in) OH	damp, nutrient-rich, also loamy soils	5 70 cm (28 in)	easy to care for
Anemone japonica hybrids Japanese anemone	LS-MA pink, white	60-100 cm (24-40 in) U	damp, humus, nutrient-rich	5 70 cm (28 in)	plant in spring, winter protection
Aquilegia caerulea hybrids columbine	LSP-ES various	60-80 cm (24-32 in) U	damp, containing humus	12 30 cm (12 in)	short-lived, allow seedheads to stand
Aruncus dioicus ☠ goat's beard	ES-MS creamy white	200 cm (80 in) U/OH	damp to moist, loamy, nutrient-rich	3 90 cm (36 in)	undemanding
Astilbe species and varieties astilbe	ES-LS red, pink, white	20-120 cm (18-48 in) U/OH	damp to moist, nutrient-rich	5-9 40-70 cm (16-28 in)	spread compost, cut back in ESP
Bergenia species and varieties	ESP-LSP red, pink, white	20-50 cm (8-20 in) U	dry to damp	7 50 cm (20 in)	spread compost
Cimicifuga ramosa bugbane, snakeroot	EA-MA creamy white	150-200 cm (60-80 in) U	damp to moist, loose, cont. humus	3 90 cm (36 in)	scented flowers
Epimedium species and varieties barrenwort, Bishop's hat	MSP-LSP various	20-35 cm (8-14 in) GC	damp to moist, permeable, humus	16 20 cm (8 in)	groundcover, partly evergreen in winter
Geranium macrorrhizum crane's bill	ES-MS red, white, pink	40 cm (16 in) GC	medium dry to damp	12-15 20-30 cm (8-12 in)	groundcover
Helleborus orientale hybrids ☠ Christmas rose	LW-MSP red, pink, white	40 cm (16 in) U/OH	cont. lime, loamy	7-9 50-70 cm (20-28 in)	cut off spotted leaves
Hosta species and varieties hosta	ES-EA white, lilac	30-70 cm (12-28 in) OH	damp, cont. humus, loamy	3-16 20-80 cm (8-32 in)	protect shoots from late frosts
Lamium maculatum deadnettle	LSP-ES red, pink, white	15-20 cm (6-8 in) GC	damp to moist, loose, nutrient-rich	15 20 cm (8 in)	groundcover
Omphalodes verna navelwort, blue-eyed Mary	LW-MSP blue, white	15 cm (6 in) GC	damp to moist, loose	16 20 cm (8 in)	spread compost, rampages
Symphytum grandiflorum	ESP-LSP light yellow, blue	30-40 cm (12-16 in) GC	damp, cont. humus	9 40 cm (16 in)	needs little care, groundcover
Tiarella cordifolia foam flower	MSP-LSP white	20 cm (8 in) GC	damp, permeable, cont. humus	16 20 cm (8 in)	groundcover
Trollius species and varieties ☠ globe flower, marsh marigold	LSP-ES yellow, orange	70 cm (28 in) U	damp to moist, cont. humus, nutrient-rich	9 40 cm (16 in)	cut back after flowering
Vinca minor lesser periwinkle	MSP-ES blue, white	15 cm (6 in) GC	medium dry to moist, loose	16 20 cm (8 in)	evergreen, ground- cover
Viola odorata sweet violet	ESP-MSP + EA lilac blue	15 cm (6 in) C	damp, loose	20 15-20 cm (6-16 in)	spreads very slowly
Waldsteinia geoides	ESP-LSP yellow	25 cm (10 in) GC	loose, nutrient- rich	16 20 cm (8 in)	spread compost or dead leaves

☠ = toxic C = cushion, OH = overhanging, GC = groundcover, R = rosette, U = upright clump, S = sub-shrub, ESP = early spring, MSP = mid spring, LSP = late spring, S = summer, A = autumn, W = winter.

Euphorbia and Hosta prefer a damp, permeable soil.

Leopard's bane.

The soil

Before planting, check the soil in your garden so that you can select suitable herbaceous plants or improve the soil if necessary. Bedding and large herbaceous plants thrive in a soil with a loose, fine, crumbly structure. A high organic material content (humus) is ideal (see p. 46). The soil should be damp to medium moist and neither acid nor alkaline.

Soil type

In order to test the soil type, take a sample of soil from a depth of about 15-20 cm (6-8 in) between your fingers and try to squeeze it.

- If the soil sifts through your fingers it is probably sandy.

- If it crumbles, it is a sandy loam.
- It is mainly loamy if you can shape it into little balls with your fingers.
- Clay can also be formed into small lumps. Pure clay feels as soft as butter.

Sandy soils are light. They contain large grains with plenty of air between them. Water will run away quickly between the sand grains and the soil will dry out easily. Herbaceous plants like pinks (*Dianthus*) and thrift (*Armeria*) will thrive on this soil. Most very large and bedding herbaceous plants will require additional doses of compost (see p. 46).

Loamy and sandy loamy soils are medium heavy soils. The soil is well aerated but can still retain sufficient water. Most herbaceous plants grow on such soils with no problems.

Clay soils are very heavy soils. They retain water well but contain less air. These soils are generally too wet for herbaceous plants. Mix the soil with coarse-grained material and enrich it with humus so that your herbaceous plants will be able to push their roots through the soil properly (see p. 46).

Degree of acidity

The pH factor of a soil will determine its degree of acidity. Follow the instructions on a tester kit which you can obtain in the gardening trade.

Depending on the requirements of individual herbaceous plants, you can distinguish three different pH ranges:

- Nearly all herbaceous plants grow on neutral soil with degrees of acidity between 5.5 and 7.
- Acid soils have pH values below 5.5 in which lupins (*Lupinus*), saxifrage (*Saxifraga x arendsii*) and iris (*Iris ensata* – also known as *Iris kaempferi*) thrive. For all other herbaceous plants, you should neutralize the soil through the addition of lime which can be obtained from your local garden centre. Use the dosage as stipulated on the packaging.
- Alkaline soils with values above 7 are ideal for all asters (*Aster*), *Leucanthemum maximum* and obedient plant (*Physostegia virginiana*). For all other herbaceous plants, improve your soil with humus (see p. 46).

Other soil tests

In addition to the soil test described above, you can also determine the nutrient content of your soil. Indicator plants will help you with this. Alternatively, you can send a sample of soil to a laboratory for testing.

Indicator plants are wild plants that will grow only on certain soils. Plants that sow themselves in your garden are, therefore, able to give you information on the quality of the soil.

For example, the large stinging nettle (*Urtica dioica*) will indicate a high level of nitrogen, while hare's foot clover (*Trifolium arvense*) grows on nutrient-poor soils.

Soil analyses are the most reliable means of soil testing. They are carried out by laboratories to which you can send samples according to their directions (look for addresses in *Yellow Pages* or ask at your local garden centre). In addition to the nutrient content, the laboratory will also determine the type of soil and degree of acidity and will give you advice on improving your soil.

Compacted and waterlogged soil

Compacted soils usually go hand in hand with waterlogging. They are found, in the main, in the gardens of newly built houses. After rain the water remains lying about in puddles and will only drain away very slowly. There is information on how to loosen up compacted soil on page 46.

Planning

In a well-balanced planting, the heights and colours of individual herbaceous plants are harmoniously combined. To achieve this result, you must consider the following points.

- The shapes of growth of the herbaceous plants (see p. 10). Set low-growing cushion and groundcover plants at the front and taller clumps in the background so that the plants do not block each other from view at flowering time.
- Early-flowering herbaceous plants, like poppies (*Papaver*) and bleeding heart (*Dicentra*), which die back after flowering. Plant these types further back in the bed. During the course of the summer, other, taller-growing species will cover up the gaps.
- Match the flower colours carefully (see p. 26). Plan your planting on paper first. You can use a staggered scheme to make best use of the different heights or distribute groups of tall and low plants all over the bed. When planting, also consider the requirements with respect to position of individual plants (see p. 12).

Making a planting plan: Make a scale drawing on graph paper of the area to be planted. Mark in areas that are shaded by trees, bushes or walls. Lay a transparent drawing sheet over the top. For every herbaceous plant, fill in the area you want it to cover in the colour of its flower.

Getting the height right

Work out a plan for plant heights and groupings depending on the shape of the bed (see p. 30) and your own personal taste.

Using perspective (illustration 1): This is suitable for a bed that is only meant to be looked at from one side. Plant the low-growing plants at the front and the taller ones at the back so that the height of growth increases gradually from the front to the back.

Cone-shaped, staggered growth (illustration 2): This is the shape to use for island beds. Plant the tallest plants in the centre, preferably using plants with a very long flowering time. Working from the centre out, gradually decrease the size of the plants.
The tall plants in the centre will prevent the onlooker from looking through it. This means that you can design the bed on all sides using different flowering times and flower colours.

1 Using perspective: *The heights of growth gradually increase from the front to the back.*

2 Cone-shaped arrangement: *Tall plants are placed in the centre; shorter ones around the edge.*

Plants with equal heights (illustration 3): These are well suited to a sloping position. Plant areas of 0.3-0.5 sq m (0.3-0.5 sq yd) with one species of the same low to medium tall herbaceous plant (see pp.16 and 17). If the heights of growth of all the plants are the same, the colours of the different flowers will form a pattern.
Exposed solitary plants (illustration 4): Design a carpet of groundcover and cushion plants (see p. 10). In between them distribute individual taller herbaceous plants, spacing them two or three times their own full-grown width apart. Overhanging clumps with year-round foliage and flowers are suitable as solitary plantings – for example, day lilies (*Hemerocallis*) or taller species of grasses.

Designing with groups of herbaceous plants

If you would prefer a looser kind of design with differing heights of plants, you can create structure in your planting by bringing in groups of taller and low-growing plants.
My tip: Taking the spacing of the plants into consideration (see pp. 16 and 17), set three or more plants of one species together in groups.
Leader plants: The tallest species of herbaceous plant will determine the choice of colour and flowering time of a plant group. The leader plant should have a conspicuous flower shape or colour. Draw the leader plants on your plan first.
Companion plants are shorter but should harmonize according to their flowering time and flower colour with the leader plant (see p. 22). Combine alternating shapes of growth, such as overhanging and upright clumps, in one group of plants. Contrasting leaf structures will also liven up the arrangement (see p. 34).
On your plan, group together three to five species of companion plants around each leader plant.

3 Plants of the same height: *Large groups of similar sized plants are very attractive on slopes.*

4 Solitary plants: *Individual plants can be planted amid groundcover plants.*

Filler plants should blend with the leader and companion plants, especially with respect to their leaf colour. Herbaceous plants with small flowers are ideal as are species with interesting leaf markings. Their flowering time may diverge from that of the leader or companion plants. Use them to fill in the remaining gaps on the graph paper.
My tip: In a large bed, you can alternate different groups of leader, companion and filler plants. Herbaceous plants that flower at the same time should harmonize in colour (see p. 26).

Day lily and campanula flower in complementary colours.

Stonecrop and autumn asters flower in autumn.

Flowers through the year

Make a decision as to whether you wish some plants always to be in flower at any one time in one bed, or whether you would prefer everything to flower at the same time. The flowering times and colours of the most popular herbaceous plants can be found on the following page and on pages 16 and 17.

NB: Depending on the weather conditions, the flowering times of your own herbaceous plants may diverge somewhat from the times given in books and on plant labels. The variety of the plant will determine the flower colour. Say which colour you want when purchasing your plants.

Large, extended areas: If you have enough room, you will be able to combine different flowering times. Distribute smaller groups of herbaceous plants that flower at the same time all over the area (see p. 23). In the foreground, reserve places for winter-flowering plants that will provide an attractive, eye-catching feature during the winter.

Smaller areas: Combine species with the same flowering times.

My tip: Extend the flowering time by choosing long-flowering herbaceous plants – for example, garden phlox (*Phlox paniculata*). You may also use herbaceous plants that flower twice (see p. 51)

Flowering time from early to late spring

Yellow and orange: *Adonis vernalis*, leopard's bane (*Doronicum orientale*, *D. plantagineum*), primrose (*Primula* species), *Waldsteinia*.
Pink to red: anemone (*Anemone blanda*), columbine (*Aquilegia* species and varieties), bleeding heart (*Dicentra spectabilis*), deadnettle (*Lamium maculatum*), primrose (*Primula* species).
Lilac to blue: anemone (*Anemone blanda*), columbine (*Aquilegia* species and varieties), *Brunnera macrophylla*, primrose (*Primula* species), lungwort (*Pulmonaria angustifolia*).
White: anemone (*Anemone blanda*), columbine (*Aquilegia* species and varieties), bleeding heart (*Dicentra spectabilis*), deadnettle (*Lamium maculatum*), primrose (*Primula* species).

Early to late summer

Yellow and orange: tickseed (*Coreopsis grandiflora*, *C. verticillata*), sunflower (*Helianthus decapetalus*), red hot poker (*Kniphofia* hybrids), loosestrife (*Lysimachia punctata*), coneflower (*Rudbeckia* species).
Pink to red: yarrow (*Achillea millefolium* hybrids), *Centaurea dealbata*, *C. montana*, pinks (*Dianthus* species), crane's bill (*Geranium* species), self-heal (*Prunella grandiflora*), lamb's ear (*Stachys grandiflora*).
Lilac to blue: anchusa (*Anchusa azurea*), campanula (*Campanula* species), *Centaurea montana*, globe thistle (*Echinops ritro*), sea holly (*Eryngium bourgatii*, *E. planum*), crane's bill (*Geranium x magnificum*, G. "Johnson's Blue"), flax (*Linum narbonense*, *L. perenne*), self-heal (*Prunella grandiflora*), scabious (*Scabiosa caucasica*), speedwell (*Veronica longifolia*, *V. spicata*).
White: yarrow (*Achillea ptarmica*), campanula (*Campanula* species), pinks (*Dianthus* species), crane's bill (*Geranium* species), Chinese loosestrife (*Lysimachia clethroides*), *Rodgersia* species.

Early to late autumn

Yellow and orange: yarrow (*Achillea filipendulina*), tickseed (*Coreopsis grandiflora*, *C. verticillata*), winter chrysanthemum (*Dendranthema indicum* hybrids), sneezewort (*Helenium* varieties), sunflower (*Helianthus decapetalus*), *Heliopsis scabra*, red hot poker (*Kniphofia* hybrids), coneflower (*Rudbeckia* species).
Pink to red: Japanese anemone (*Anemone huphensis*, *A. japonica*), Michaelmas daisies (*Aster novi-belgii*, *A. dumosus*, *A. novae-angliae*), chrysanthemum (*Dendranthema indicum* hybrids), stonecrop (*Sedum spectabile*, *S. telephium*),
Lilac to blue: Michaelmas daisy (*Aster novi-belgii*, *A. dumosus*, *A. novae angliae*), *Ceratostigma plumbagino-ides*.
White: Japanese anemone (*Anemone huphensis*, *A. japonica*), Michaelmas daisy (*Aster novi-belgii*, *A. dumosus*, *A. novae-angliae*), bugbane (snakeroot) (*Cimicifuga* species), chrysanthemum (*Dendranthema indicum* hybrids).

Early to late winter

Yellow and orange: primrose (*Primula vulgaris*).
Pink to red: cyclamen (*Cyclamen coum*), Christmas rose (*Helleborus orientalis*), primrose (*Primula vulgaris*), red lungwort (*Pulmonaria rubra*).
Lilac to blue: primrose (*Primula vulgaris*), violet (*Viola odorata*).
White: cyclamen (*Cyclamen coum*), Christmas rose (*Helleborus niger*), primrose (*Primula vulgaris*).

Designing herbaceous beds

By using herbaceous plants you will be able to create very imaginative beds to show off the splendid flowers, fascinating leaves, interesting shapes of growth and varying heights of the different plants. The following pages contain a host of ideas and design suggestions – for example, multi-coloured plantings, beds that use only different shades of one colour and wild plantings that replicate nature.

Left: Several subtle colours are harmoniously blended in this summery herbaceous garden.
Top: The red coneflower prefers a sunny position.

Combining colours

Colours that stand out are an important basic element of design. The main colour in a garden is usually green which is the colour of leaves. Apart from that, the entire palette of colours, in the finest of different shades, is at your disposal. In order to create interesting, atmospheric schemes, you can combine complementary colours, colour trios or a range of shades of one basic colour (see p. 27). Using these combinations will ensure that the colours in your herbaceous bed will harmonize. If you have already had some experience of combining colours, you can experiment further by combining colours based on these rules. Make sure that the herbaceous plants you wish to use to create a particular effect do, in fact, all flower at the same time (see p. 22).

Creating moods with colour

Colours can enhance different moods in the observer and can even be used to create a particular atmosphere.

- Blue is a cool colour. Blue flowers look unusual and interesting.
- Lilac and violet are shades of blue mixed with shades of red. The more red there is in the shade, the more warmth it transmits.
- Pink is a romantic colour.
- Red and orange are the colours of fire. They are warm colours that will enliven a herbaceous planting.
- Yellow has a light, glowing effect. Even on cloudy days a bed of yellow flowers may conjure up sunshine in your garden.
- White creates an elegant, distanced, slightly cool atmosphere.
- Green is the colour of foliage. It has a tranquillizing, calming effect.

The atmosphere or mood created by a colour becomes most noticeable in a bed of one single colour (see p. 33). If you combine several colours in a planting, the mood of the most dominant colour will prevail. In the same way, the introduction of a new colour can change the mood completely.

Seasons and colours

In every season certain colours predominate in nature and in the garden. If you select these colours as the flower colours of your herbaceous plants, they will blend happily into their surroundings and the effect you wish to create will be enhanced. You can, however, consciously decide to combine other colours. For example, you could contrast stronger colours with delicate pastel shades or vice versa.

Spring: Delicate pastel shades of both leaves and flowers generally determine the effect of the garden. Further into the year, the shades of colour become stronger. The soft colours of white rock cress *(Arabis caucasica*) and navelwort (*Omphalodes verna*) enhance the feeling of lightness after a cold winter.

If you prefer the stronger colours typical of summer, choose glowing colours like golden yellow, purple and violet. Brilliant colours can be introduced to the springtime bed with aubrieta, leopard's bane (*Doronicum*) and *Alyssum*.

Early summer: Both in nature and in the garden, strong, glowing colours now predominate. The fiery red of poppies (*Papaver orientale*), the clear blue of *Delphinium* and the carmine red of *Astilbe* are typical. Shades of blue will create an almost mystical mood at dusk. You could also combine the subtle pastel shades of pinks (*Dianthus*), *Gypsophila* and phlox instead of stronger colours to create a summery, romantic herbaceous border that will enchant all who see it.

Late summer: The warmth of summer can be reflected in yellow, orange and brownish-red tones in the herbaceous border. This warmth is provided by day lilies (*Hemerocallis*), *Heliopsis*,

The colour wheel

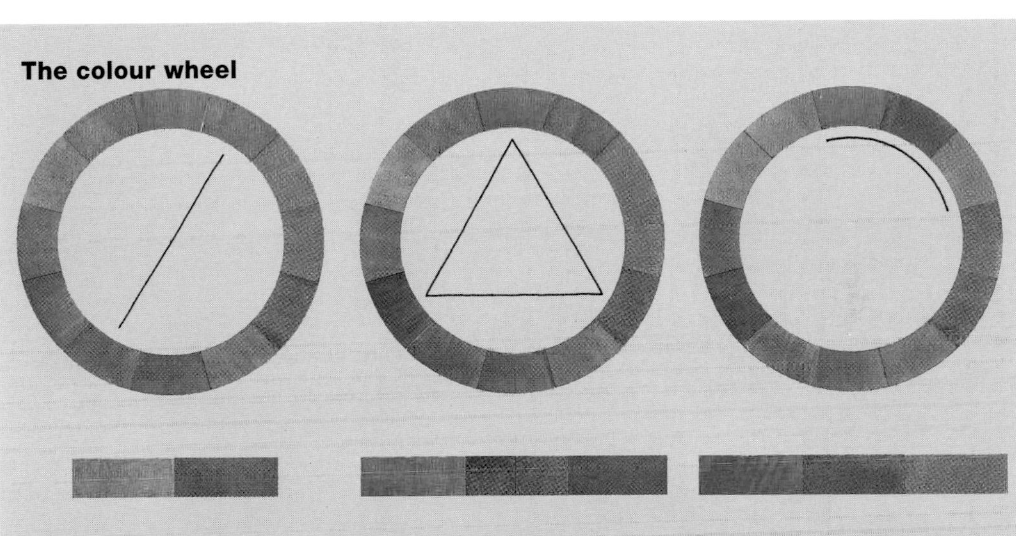

On a colour wheel, around which colours have been distributed according to how they shade into each other, ***the complementary colours*** are situated opposite each other. They boost each other and gain in brilliance. Examples of this effect are red and green, lilac and yellow or blue and orange.

Colour trios are formed by three colours that contrast strongly and are sited furthest apart on the colour circle. The corners of an equilateral triangle laid across the colour circle will highlight colour trios such as yellow, blue and red.

Runs of similar colours are produced by colours that lie side by side on the colour circle. The gentle transition from shade to shade ensures that the colours will harmonize well. One example of a colour run is provided by the colours yellow, orange-yellow and orange shown here.

sneezewort (*Helenium*), yarrow (*Achillea*), coneflower (*Rudbeckia*) and red hot poker (*Kniphofia* hybrids). The continuously flowering members of this selection will form a seamless transition of colour right through into golden October and will mirror the colours of autumnal trees nearby.
During an Indian summer you can also ensure a few more shades of pink and rose in your garden with Michaelmas daisies (*Aster*), autumn anemone (*Anemone*) and stonecrop (*Sedum telphium*). In this way, colour accents can be introduced among the more subtle tones of autumn.

A final check

When planning your colour schemes do remember to lift your eyes from the flowerbeds and look around to see what other colours will contrast with those of your herbaceous plants. A vivid pattern on garden furniture or a painted wall can completely spoil the effect you are trying to create.

White flowers soften the strong colour contrasts in this bed.

Colourful beds

A colourful herbaceous bed or border planted with contrasting colours that are clearly delimited one from another has an enlivening, cheerful effect. Alternatively, you can also combine similar flower colours in one bed. Such a bed will appear harmonious and elegant in its fine gradations of colour.

Combining flower colours: In order to prevent the bed from becoming a jumble of colours, stick to just a few colours. The three colours of a colour trio, two complementary colours or one colour run (see p. 27) will be quite sufficient. You may also add a few white-flowering plants, which will soften the hard colour contrasts. However, the be-all and end-all of colour combining is achieving simultaneous flowering times.

My tip: In a larger bed, herbaceous plants that flower simultaneously need not all stand close together. If they complement each other in different parts of the bed, the planting will be given a proper framework and form a complete unit.

The right colours for every bed

Consider the following points when making your choice of colours, so that your herbaceous border will blend harmoniously into its surroundings.
The size of the bed: Strong colours are best suited to small nooks in full sunlight. Here, you can plant blue campanula (*Campanula*) and orange-red day lilies (*Hemerocallis* hybrids) together (see p. 22). These two species will flower from early to late summer in brilliant colours. For larger areas, choose more subtle shades. Glowing colours are difficult to combine in large areas because of their rather intense effect. Pastel shades will create a harmonious effect in all combinations of colour. In a large, sunny bed, you could, for example, combine the summer-flowering lady's mantle (*Alchemilla*), lamb's ear (*Stachys byzantina*) and sea holly (*Eryngium*). If you set a few stonecrop (*Sedum spectabile*) and asters (*Aster dumosus*) between them, the bed will delight with another flowering highlight in the autumn (see p. 22).
The size of the garden: Brilliant colours, particularly red, will appear to make points that are further away seem closer. This means that such colours are clear even at a distance but also have a constricting effect. For this reason, be sparing with intense colours in a small garden. Pastel shades appear to vanish against the sky, dissolve boundaries and thereby manage to make small gardens look larger.
The surroundings of a bed: In a varied garden design, a more subtle range of colours in a herbaceous bed will have a calming effect and will make smaller areas appear larger. Choose colour runs for the flower colours (see p. 26). Large, solitary plants will be particularly effective. In a semi-shady bed, for example, early-summer-flowering plants, like *Aquilegia* hybrids, crane's bill *(Geranium himalayense*), cornflower (*Centaurea*) and primula (*Primula denticulata*), in shades of blue, lilac, pink and white are very attractive.
My tip: A colourful bed of herbaceous plants like *Delphinium*, *Phlox paniculata* and large poppies (*Papaver orientale*) is reminiscent of a cottage garden. You can further underline this rustic character with colourful roses (see p. 40).

Softening effects

Strong colour contrasts can look rather hard in bright sunlight. These contrasts can be softened with the use of white-flowering plants or herbaceous plants with light-coloured leaves. These softening elements can also be used to create a balance if certain strong colours do not go together too well.
Small-flowering plants like baby's breath (*Gypsophila*) and white valerian (*Centranthus*) lighten up their surroundings. Herbaceous plants with light-coloured foliage can act as a softener throughout the whole season.
Grey-leafed herbaceous plants are suitable for sunny positions – for example, lamb's ears (*Stachys*), mugwort (*Artemisia*) and lavender (*Lavandula*). In shady positions, softeners create an effect of more light, and neighbouring flowers will regain the brilllance that has been lost in the shadows. Herbaceous plants with yellow-green or white-green variegated leaves, like *Hosta*, dead nettle (*Lamium maculatum*) or lungwort (*Pulmonaria*), also lighten up their surroundings.

Planning the shapes of beds

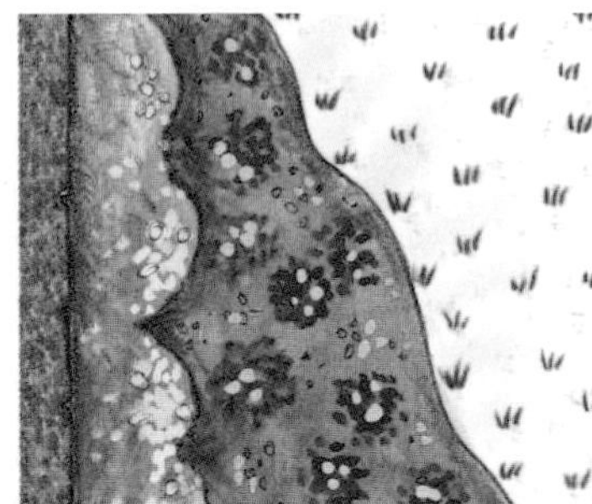

2 A wide ***border*** *is suitable for a front garden, a house wall, a sitting area or the edge of a lawn.*

The shape of a bed will influence its possibilities for design, so give yourself plenty of time at the planning stage. Take into consideration whether your bed is in a front garden, along a house wall, in the centre of a lawn or bordering the edge of a lawn.

Garden areas

(illustration 3)

Lawn: Break up the effect of a large lawn with island beds. You can also create borders around a lawn. You can have either straight or curved edges between the lawn and the bed.
Front garden: A wide herbaceous border may frame a house entrance most effectively. If the front garden lies to the south of the house, it is usually very sunny. A front garden in any other position will be semi-sunny or shady. Try grouping together plants that flower at different times of the year (see p. 23) so that some plants are always in flower at each point.
House wall: A narrow border may provide a link from a lawn or path in front of the house to climbing plants on the house wall.
My tip: Warmth-loving, grey-leafed herbaceous plants will do well on a south wall.

1 A bed on a slope: *You can plant herbaceous plants on any slope – for example, on a slope under a raised patio.*

Garden path: Narrow borders to the right and left of paths are ideal for cushion and scented herbaceous plants. As you pass by on a sunny day, you will catch their pleasant aromas.
Sitting area: A herbaceous border beside a sitting area can serve as a visual or wind screen. The plants will also give visual pleasure on long summer evenings or provide you with lovely scents as dusk falls (see p.40). To lighten up the total effect, employ white summer-flowering herbaceous plants (see p. 32). Tall, dense-growing plants, such as coneflower (*Rudbeckia nitida*), will provide both a visual screen and shelter from the wind.

Basic shapes

(illustrations 1, 2 and 4)

Herbaceous beds can be constructed as narrow or wide borders, island or peninsular beds.
Narrow borders: Create a 1-1.5 m (40-60 in) wide bed that is viewed from one side only. In order to extend the bed visually, use a skilfully staggered arrangement of heights (see p. 20) and colour runs (see p. 26) as similar shades will attract the attention of the observer to the structure of leaves and flowers.
This concentration on detail will make the bed appear larger.
Wide border (illustration 2): Do not waste space even in a bed that is wider than

1.50 m (60 in). Choose herbaceous plants that can be cleverly combined in groups (see p. 21).
If the border is a long one, it will be easier to plan if you repeat a particular planting pattern using the same species or mirror it at intervals along an imaginary line in the bed. This will also help the planting arrangement to hold together.
My tip: Heap up the soil to create a mound. This will open up new possibilities for combining tall and low-growing herbaceous plants.
Island bed (illustration 4): You need to be able to walk all around it, so this bed should be situated in the middle of a lawn or paved area. Choose a round, angular or completely irregular shape that will blend well with the surroundings. Aim for a cone-shaped arrangement when planting (see p. 20).
Peninsular bed: This should project out into the lawn. The edge at the back can be formed by a hedge or a fence.

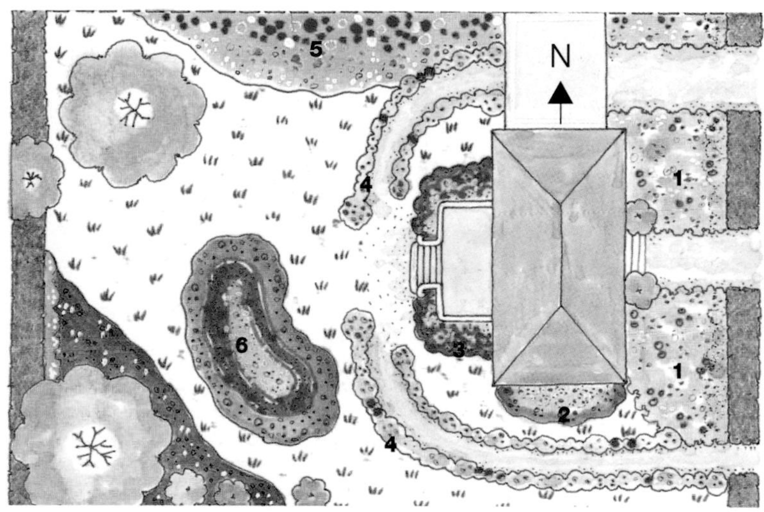

3 A garden plan: *Herbaceous borders can be built – 1 in a front garden; 2 along a house wall; 3 beside a sitting area; 4 along a garden path; 5 along the edges of lawns. Island beds look good in large areas of lawn (6).*

A peninsular bed takes up a little less space than an island bed. Here, again, choose a basically cone-shaped arrangement of plant heights (see p. 20).
A bed on a slope (see illustration 1): When planted on a slope herbaceous plants prevent soil erosion by holding it firmly in their roots. Plant mainly herbaceous plants of the same height (see p. 21). You can also add a few interesting features such as large stones. The right colour and shape of a stone can contrast effectively with leaf and flower colours and shapes.

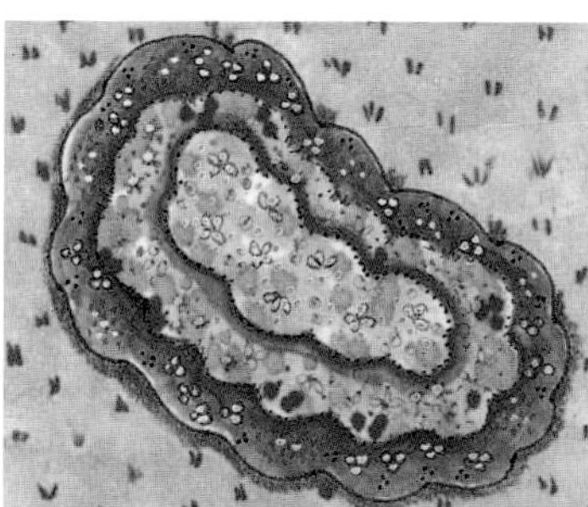
4 An island bed *can be walked around and will break up a large area of lawn.*

Designing herbaceous beds

A herbaceous bed planted all in white is very effective. Included here are Veronica virginica "Alba", Monarda "Schneewittchen", Phlox paniculata "Pax", Verbascum chaixii "Album", Physostegia virginiana "Summer Snow", Artemisia ludoviviana and Achillea ptarmica.

Designing in several shades of one colour

The plants of a single-colour planting flower in many shades of one colour underlined only by the green of the foliage. This sort of arrangement looks very elegant as the predominating colour can appear very intense (see p. 26). Choose a colour that you particularly like and which has many shades, both pale and striking. Also make sure that the colour will go well with its surroundings and with neighbouring plants.
Once you have decided on a flower colour, look for suitable herbaceous plants. The calendar of flowering times (see p. 23) will help you in this. Further information on individual herbaceous plant varieties can be found in catalogues from plant nurseries. The plants should all flower at the same time for the single-colour bed to achieve its full effect. Check the flowering times carefully.
My tip: A bed in which you keep to lighter colours will appear fresher if you mix in a few stronger shades of the same colour. For example, a bed in shades of pink will be enhanced with a few dark pink flowers.

Creative designs

In single-colour combinations, the structures of the individual herbaceous plants become more important. This includes the height of growth, the patterning of the leaves and the shape of individual flowers.
Height of growth: To liven up the bed, combine herbaceous plants with different heights of growth. An interesting effect is achieved by a staggered arrangement of heights or a cone-like arrangement (see p. 20).
Leaf patterns: A few herbaceous plants with decorative foliage will add variety to the bed (see p. 34). If the flowers of a particular herbaceous plant with interesting leaves are of the wrong colour for your arrangement, its flowering time must vary from that of the other herbaceous plants in order to avoid destroying the effect of the single-colour bed.
Flower shapes: The more varied the shapes of the flowers, the more fascinating their effect. Combine plants with daisy-shaped flowers – for example, autumn asters (*Aster*) and *Heliopsis*, with the bell-shaped flowers of campanula (*Campanula*) and balloon flower (*Platycodon*). Beside these classic herbaceous plants, more bizarre plants like bergamot (*Monarda* hybrids), globe thistle (*Echinops*) and sea holly (*Eryngium*) are very effective.
My tip: *Gypsophila*-like plants form a very regular background to a herbaceous border. In order to disguise an unattractive hedge or garage wall, for example, place baby's breath (*Gypsophila*) or *Boltonia asteroides* behind the other herbaceous plants in your border.

Single-colour combinations

Brilliant golden yellow, flowering time in late summer, sunny positions: tickseed (*Coreopsis verticilata*), evening primrose (*Oenothera tetragona*), yarrow (*Achillea filipendulina*).
Purple to pink, flowering time early autumn to middle of autumn, sunny positions: autumn anemone (*Anemone japonica* hybrids), autumn asters (*Aster novae-angliae*), stonecrop (*Sedum telephium*)
Lilac/blue, flowering time middle of spring to late spring, semi-shady to shady positions: blue bugle (*Ajuga reptans*), columbine (*Aquilegia vulgaris*), lungwort (*Pulmonaria saccharata*).
White, flowering time middle of summer, semi-shady to shady positions: monkshood (*Aconitum napellus* "Album"), *Astilbe*, crane's bill (*Geranium macrorrhizum*), *Hosta*.

Designing herbaceous beds

Herbaceous plants do not enchant only with their splendid flowers; many of the leaves are also very decorative. The leaves provide a great variety of shapes, colours and sizes.
The sizes of leaves range from a few millimetres in the case of thyme (Thymus) right through to plate-size in Rodgersia. The feathery leaves of mugwort (Artemisia) look very pretty beside the large, wide leaves of Hosta.
The colours of the foliage may vary from light yellow-green to shades of dark green. The leaves may even be silvery, bluish or reddish. The red-brown foliage of Heuchera micrantha is very attractive. A highlight among this colour play is provided by the patterns on foliage as seen in Hosta and lungwort (Pulmonaria saccarata).

Heuchera micrantha.

Pulmonaria saccharata.

Thymus x citriodorus.

Artemisia canascens.

Ligularia dentata "Othello".

A herbaceous border can look very decorative even without any flowers.

Leaves can provide additional highlights in the autumn and winter. Barrenwort (Epimedium) and Bergenia display attractive autumnal colouring. The winter green and evergreen herbaceous plants (see p. 6) retain their foliage in winter. Enchanting scenes are created when the leaves become covered with rime or snow on frosty winter days.

Decorative leaves for all seasons

Hosta fortunei.

Ajuga reptans "Atropurpurea".

A mixed border

The mixed border is a common feature in many gardens. Among the herbaceous plants you will also find shrubs, summer annuals and bulbous and tuberous plants, all in a single wide bed. This very natural-looking but none the less carefully planned mixture of different plant types is what gives the mixed border its particular charm.
Because of the great variety of plant shapes and types, the mixed border looks attractive at all times of the year. In early spring the first bulbous and tuberous plants will be in flower and, in winter, the shrubs provide interest with their bark, fruit and leaves.
A special feature of the mixed border is its own internal growing cycle. Over the course of a year, consecutive seedlings appear one after the other to fill the gaps.

Planning a mixed border

Space required: In order to prevent herbaceous and woody plants smothering each other you should start with a strip that is at least 2-3 m (7-10 ft) wide and 5 m (17 ft) long.
Choosing shrubs: Start with a selection of shrubs that will form the framework of the border. Consult tree nursery catalogues and other helpful literature and consider the colour harmony of flowers and leaves (see p. 26). Also consider the position requirements, flowering times and mature heights of the shrubs. The optimal height is between 1.5 and 4 m (5-13 ft). Also make a note of each shrub's final width and the correct spacing between shrubs.
Making a planting plan: Making a plan on paper is absolutely essential when creating a successful mixed border (see p. 20).
Draw in the shrubs as circles with their diameter representing the width of the mature shrubs. Use two to three times the required plant spacing, so that there will be plenty of room for the herbaceous plants. Also consider the areas that will be shaded by the shrubs on your plan.
My tip: If you are not too sure about your ability to plan the bed, seek advice from a landscape gardener or from your local garden centre.
Choosing leafy plants: Choose leafy plants that will harmonize with the flowering time, flower colour and foliage colour of the shrubs. Information on summer flowers, bulbous and tuberous plants can be obtained from nursery catalogues, at nurseries and garden centres and from books and magazines.
Forming groups: Put together small plant groups (see p. 21). Treat the shrubs like leader plants and harmonize the flower and leaf colours of the leafy plants with them. Taller leafy plants should be employed like companion plants and their flowering times should coincide with those of the shrubs. Low-growing, leafy plants should be used like filler plants.
NB: Keep to the correct spacing for shrubs planted between leafy and woody plants. Overhanging bushes can be underplanted with ground-cover or cushion plants.
My tip: You will create an effective framework and an integrated, harmonious whole if you are use the same individual species in several different parts of the bed.

Ideas for planting combinations

There follow a few ideas for combinations that should help you to create effective planting groups.

- With spiraea (*Spiraea japonica*), which produces flowers of purple-red in summer, match the blue cushions of catmint (*Napeta faasenii* "Six Hills Giant"). In late summer, just as the catmint is flowering for the last time, plant low-growing, orange pompon dahlias (*Dahlia*) to create a dash of colour.
- A spring-time trio in golden yellow and blue is created by *Forsythia x intermedia* with an

In the spring, azaleas, forget-me-nots and tulips bloom in this mixed border.

underplanted carpet of yellow-flowering *Waldsteinia geoides* that can be broken up with a few clumps of *Hyazinthoides hispanica*.

- Witch hazel (*Hamamelis*) is an attractive winter-flowering shrub. In the summer, the dark green foliage of this shrub provides a decorative background for a combination of yellow coneflower (*Rudbeckia fulgida*) and violet-blue summer sage (*Salvia nemorosa*). The following summer flowers will also complement this shrub: lilac *Verbena rigida*, yellow-orange cosmea (*Cosmos sulphureus*) and yellow *Zinnia elegans*.

Study the experts

On visits to gardens that are open to the public, take with you either a camera or a notebook and try to find particularly pleasing mixed borders. You do not have to copy these exactly in your own garden but you should learn a lot by trying to assess exactly why these particular planting arrangements are so successful. This will then help you to create borders that are just as effective.

Designing herbaceous beds

You will be able to find wonderful wild flowers to grow in nature-garden plantings. Try blending the beautiful colours of sage (Salvia nemorosa), catmint (Napeta) and valerian (Centranthus). Mix the individual species thoroughly when planting them. After a few years they will have formed exquisite natural-looking groups.

Natural-looking herbaceous plantings

You will find a wide selection of wild herbaceous plants in any plant nursery. These are pure species which have originated directly from nature and were not cultivated. By planting them in your flowerbed you will be bringing a little bit of nature into the garden which will look absolutely perfect in a romantic nook. In this way you will be able to recreate a glimpse of natural-looking fringes of woodland as well as sunny fields or hillsides. Provided the conditions in your garden are identical to the natural conditions preferred by these plants, you will not even need to fertilize, weed, hoe or water after the first year. Do not remove any dead plant parts as, when they decay, they will improve the structure of the soil. In addition, you can also offer rare herbaceous plants survival space in a natural planting and thus protect endangered species.

My tip: In order to ensure that the wild herbaceous plants develop into a balanced ecosystem, choose a herbaceous plant community that is adapted to the conditions on site. A plant community consists of species of herbaceous plants that would naturally grow together in locations with similar conditions in the wild.

Planning the planting

Designing the beds: Compared with the cultivated forms and varieties, wild herbaceous plants usually have more subtle colours and smaller flowers. Colour design plays a lesser role with these plants. To give the planting a natural-looking character, distribute plants with different heights freely over the bed. Plant in groups of about three to five specimens of each species and mix the individual species thoroughly.

My tip: Strew the surface of the bed with individual larger stones or rocks and tree roots to form a miniature landscape.

Improving the soil: Most wild herbaceous plants are adapted to nutrient-poor soils. Test the nutrient content of your soil (see p. 19). If it is too rich, you can remove nutrients from the soil by sowing quick and densely growing plants like nasturtium (*Tropaeolum*) and phacelia (*Phacelia*) on the area in spring or summer. After about two months, when the plants have grown into a dense mat of plant cover, pull the plants out by their roots. You can let this plant matter rot on the compost heap.

Suitable wild herbaceous plants

Woodland edge: The following plants are well adapted to the conditions of nutrients and light found underneath trees and bushes (see p. 13): monkshood (*Aconitum*), baneberry (*Actaea*), windflowers (*Anemone nemorosa*), *Campanula latifolia*, lily-of-the-valley (*Convallaria*), foxglove (*Digitalis*), hemp agrimony (*Eupatorium*), loosestrife (*Lysimachia*), comfrey (*Symphytum*), meadow rue (*Thalictrum*), ferns, bugle (*Ajuga reptans*), crane's bill (*Geranium*), hellebore (*Helleborus*), Solomon's seal (*Polygonatum*), lungwort (*Pulmonaria*), violets (*Viola odorata*) and columbine (*Aquilegia*).

Open spaces: On open, sunny spaces the following will thrive: cat's ear (*Antennaria*), asters (*Aster*), cornflower (*Centaurea*), globe thistle (*Echinops*), spurge (*Euphorbia*), statice (*Limonium*), catmint (*Napeta*), sage (*Salvia*), stonecrop (*Sedum*), germander (*Teucrium*), thyme (*Thymus*), mullein (*Verbascum*), valerian (*Centranthus*) and marsh marigold (*Trollius*).

Roses and herbaceous plants seek to outdo each other in this wonderful summer garden.

Scented herbaceous plants

Have you ever suddenly found yourself thinking of Provence while in your garden? If so this was probably when a cloud of scent from thyme (*Thymus*) or lavender (*Lavandula*) wafted past your nose. Scented plants will enrich any herbaceous bed. Plant them along the front of the beds, along paths or directly beside a sitting area in order to enjoy the scent. Herbaceous plants with a similar scent can be combined in groups. In the case of plants with a spicy aroma, it is the leaves that are scented, while it is the flowers of sweet- or fruity-smelling plants that release perfume. Check the flowering times before combining plants.

- A sweet, flowery scent is produced by *Phlox paniculata*, peonies (*Paeonia lactiflora*) and day lily (Hemerocallis).
- A fruity, fresh scent is provided by bugbane (snakeroot) (*Cimicifuga ramosa*) and *Hosta plantaginea*.
- A herby-spicy scent is released by thyme (*Thymus*) and bergamot (*Monarda*).

Herbaceous plants as cut flowers

Although you can admire your herbaceous plants in the garden, you can also cut them and combine them in decorative bunches in a vase. These bouquets are ideal as a present or for decorating your living room, although some herbaceous plants wilt quickly if put in a vase. Long-lasting flowers include yarrow (*Achillea*), monkshood (*Aconitum*), *Leucanthemum*, *Gypsophila*, *Heliopsis*, sneezewort (*Helenium*), peony (*Paeonia*) and marsh marigold (*Trollius*).
Add a few interesting leaves to liven up your bouquets. Take them from *Bergenla*, *Hosta* and lady's mantle (*Alchemilla*).
My tip: If you are going to use the border for producing cut flowers, remove them carefully from the back so that the gaps are not so obvious. It ls better to grow individual herbaceous plants for cutting in a vegetable garden or some other inconspicuous place.

Herbaceous plants and roses

Roses and herbaceous plants complement each other in two ways. While summer-flowering herbaceous plants will flower simultaneously with the roses, the spring- and autumn-flowering ones (see p. 22) will provide colour in the garden both before and after the roses have bloomed.
As roses often create a very intense effect, companion plants should be in more subtle colours or should perfectly complement the colour of the rose flowers. Blue delphinium (*Delphinium*) harmonizes well with most rose flowers.
The following plants make good companion plants for roses: *Campanula*, *Gypsophila*, lavender (*Lavandula*), catmint (*Nepeta x faassenii*) and *Phlox paniculata*.

Grasses and ferns

Grasses and ferns are listed among the herbaceous plants but they form a separate group as they do not produce colourful flowers. With their longish leaves and interesting flower and seedhead shapes, grasses will enhance any flowerbed. Taller species, like *Miscanthus* and *Pennisetum*, can even be planted as leader plants (see p. 21), while smaller grasses, like *Festuca glauca* or *Bouteloua gracilis*, make decorative companion or filler plants. You can choose grasses for sunny, semi-shady or shady positions. Ferns, on the other hand, being forest-dwelling plants, prefer semi-shady and shady positions. Pretty species with decorative leaves include *Mattheucia strutiopteris* and *Phyllitis scolopendrium*.

Herbaceous plants in large containers and pots

Herbaceous plants in attractive containers can be used to decorate gardens, balconies or patios. Plants in containers look good along paths or in a herbaceous border. You can also fill up gaps in a plant border with pots. When adding a container to an established planting, choose herbaceous plants with attractive foliage (see p. 34) so that the container will look good for a long time.
There are several points to consider.

- Use frost-proof pots. Check this before you buy.
- Consider the light conditions. Shade-loving plants will not turn into sun-worshippers when planted in pots.
- Do not plant herbaceous plants with long, deep roots in pots as the space will be too cramped.

The following are suitable for planting in pots: *Astilbe*, *Artemisia*, *Hosta*, poppy (*Papaver nudicaule*) and stonecrop (*Sedum*).

Caring for herbaceous plants

Planting and care

In the right position, and with adequate care, herbaceous plants will thrive and produce splendid flowers. The following pages will tell you all that you need to know to enjoy many years of beautiful flowers in your own, personally designed herbaceous bed or border.

Left: The warm autumn light creates an enchanted moment in this herbaceous bed.
Top: The day lily (Hemerocallis hybrid "Goldarama") flowers in glowing yellow-orange in summer.

Buying herbaceous plants

You will find a wide selection of herbaceous plants in garden centres, street markets and specialist herbaceous plant nurseries. If you want to be sure of buying plants of good quality, however, you really should go to a reputable garden centre or order them by mail order from a specialist nursery. Such sources should provide you with strong, healthy plants plus advice on how to plant them and their preferred conditions with reference to light, soil and nutrients. If you buy your plants from a nursery near where you live, you will usually find that they have a large selection of plants that should grow well in the prevailing conditions in your area. Check the plants carefully before buying them.
Healthy herbaceous plants are recognizable by the following characteristics:

- healthy foliage without spots, eaten parts or crippled parts;
- numerous shoots;
- a dense rootstock, in which can be seen light-coloured, young root tips.

Avoid buying young plants already in flower or else cut off the flowers. The strength the plant uses to produce flowers and seeds will be at the cost of growth.
As an alternative to going to your local nursery, consult *Yellow Pages* to find the names and addresses of specialist herbaceous plant nurseries that supply plants by mail order.

Plant spacing and numbers of plants

Herbaceous plants are usually young, and therefore small, when you buy them and will increasingly crowd each other as they grow if they are planted too close together. For this reason, you should observe the correct spacing recommended for individual species, depending on their shape of growth. Herbaceous plants that produce rhizomes spread over larger areas than those with single shoots.
Recommended planting spacings can be found in the table on pages 16 and 17.
NB: If you plant herbaceous plants with different spacing requirements next to each other, always go by the larger spacing.
My tip: It is better to plant herbaceous plants further apart than too close together. Spaces that are too large can be filled in later with additional planting.
How many plants: On your planting plan, draw in all the herbaceous plants with the correct spacing (see p. 20). If you choose a different symbol for each species, and make a proper key indicating which symbol is used for which plant, you will easily be able to estimate how many herbaceous plants of each variety you will need. The best idea then is to make a shopping list so that you do not forget any.

Planting time

The best time for planting is spring but most species of herbaceous plants can be planted in spring or autumn. Plants that should not be planted in the autumn include autumn chrysanthemum (*Dendrathema indicum* hybrids), red hot poker (*Knephofia*), lavender (*Lavandula*), catmint (*Napeta x faassenii*), rock rose (*Helianthemum*) and other autumn-flowering plants as well as grasses and ferns.
Planting in spring: The best planting time is in the first and second months of spring. After the winter rest period, the plants will root well when they start growing again and will develop quickly. Only *Hosta* is sensitive to late frosts.
Planting in autumn: At this time, most herbaceous plant nurseries have a plentiful selection. Plant during early to mid autumn so that all of the herbaceous plants will have taken root before the first frosts. The herbaceous plants may require winter protection from now on – for example, a covering of conifer branches (see p. 52).

Before you buy any plants make sure that they are healthy so that you will be able to enjoy them for a long time. The rootstock should be dense and firmly rooted in the soil in the pot. A healthy herbaceous plant has numerous shoots and the leaves should not show any marks, traces of having been eaten by insects or crippled growth.

Preparing the soil

Before starting to plant, check your soil (see p.18). Bedding plants prefer loose, humus-rich soils. Carefully remove any weeds so that no pieces of root remain in the soil. Most garden soils require only superficial loosening and some enriching with humus. Start the work in the autumn if you want to plant in the spring. For autumn planting, start two months earlier. Very dense, compacted soils will require special treatment, as will heavy or sandy soils.
Normal soils are best loosened in the autumn. Dig over to one spade's depth down and allow the soil to lie like this over the winter. You can rake it smooth again in the spring.

Increasing the humus content

Humus is the organic substance of the soil. It provides nutrients, encourages beneficial organisms and helps to create a looser soil structure.
In order to increase the humus content, distribute a 5-10 cm (2-4 in) layer of bark compost, ripe garden compost or autumn leaves between the herbaceous plants.

Loosening compacted soils

Dig over compacted soil to two spades' depth. If the humus or nutrient content is low, you can sow green fertilizer plants beforehand.
Green fertilizer plants: The deep roots of these plants will loosen up the soil. Sow plants such as *Phacelia* or mustard (*Sinapis*) around mid summer. Then dig over the soil two weeks before planting, to one spade's depth. This will provide additional nutrients for the plants. *Papilionaceae* like lupins (*Lupinus*) will enrich the soil with nitrogen.
Deep digging: Remove the top layer of soil to one spade's depth. Then loosen the lower layer to a further 30 cm (12 in) depth with a garden fork. Now replace the top soil.
My tip: Put the top layer of soil into a wheelbarrow while loosening the lower layer.

Improving heavy and sandy soils

Heavy soils should be loosened by mixing sand or grit to one spade's depth into the soil. You should also increase the humus content.
Sandy soils can be improved by working in a 5-10 cm (2-4 in) layer of compost. This will improve the soil structure and increase the nutrient content.

Planting herbaceous plants

The day before planting, rake the prepared soil smooth. You can work in a mineral-rich compound fertilizer while doing this (see p. 48). Immediately before planting, stand the plants, still in their pots, in a water-filled bath for two hours so that they can absorb plenty of water.
Unpotting: Tapping the edge of the pot once firmly on the edge of a table or something similar will loosen the rootstock. Try not to tear off any roots that may be protruding from the hole in the bottom of the pot. If the rootstock will not come out easily, you can cut open a plastic pot with scissors. Also cut open biodegradable pots so that the roots can spread out into the soil.
Planting

- Use a wooden plank as a walkway and to protect the soil.
- Distribute the prepared plants over the bed according to your planting plan (see p. 20).
- Dig a hole for each plant with a trowel.
- There must be room in the hole for the rootstock to fit in properly and the plant should end up sitting no deeper than it was in the pot.
- Hold the rootstock in the hole so that the roots hang down loosely.
- Fill the hole with soil.
- Press the rootstock down

Prepare the soil carefully so that your herbaceous plants will thrive.

firmly with both hands.

● When all plants have been planted, water the soil thoroughly.

Protecting the soil

The soil is a living unit. The sun and wind will dry it out and constant treading on it will compact it.

A layer of mulch will protect it from sunlight and drying out. Use bark from a garden centre or your own garden compost.

An orange-brown day lily.

Your herbaceous plants will require nutrients in the form of fertilizer if they are to grow and thrive.

Fertilizing

The annual growth of new shoots, a profusion of flowers and the production of fruit require plenty of nutrients. By cutting back and removing deadheads, we prevent nutrients contained in the plants from returning to the soil through decomposition. This means that minerals and other nutrients have to be introduced through regular applications of fertilizer, particularly nitrogen, phosphorus, potassium, iron, magnesium and sulphur.

Note: Wild herbaceous plantings do not require added fertilizer as the bed will supply itself with this when dead plant parts decompose in the soil.

Types of fertilizer

Organic fertilizers are made up of plant and animal components. Mineral fertilizers are artificially produced.

Organic fertilizers and mineral fertilizers have a balanced ratio of nutrients.

Specific mineral fertilizers should only be used on expert advice after a soil analysis (see p. 18).

NB: A plant that produces many leaves and flowers will require more fertilizer than a plant with fewer leaves.

Organic fertilizers take a long time to release nutrients for absorption by plants.

The most suitable and cheapest fertilizer for bedding plants is garden compost. You can ulitize it after it has rotted for five months. Special composting bins can be bought in which kitchen plant refuse can be composted as well as garden refuse such as clippings. In the autumn, spread a 10cm (4 in) thick layer of compost between the herbaceous plants. Compost will also provide the soil with humus (see p. 18).

If you have no compost of your own, you can also use hoof and horn meal from the gardening trade. Use the dosage according to the instructions on the packaging. In view of the worry about BSE (mad cow disease) in recent years, it is probably inadvisable to use blood or bonemeal unless it comes from a very reputable source. Even then, wear gloves and a mask when handling it and make sure that children do not have access to it.

My tip: Organic fertilizers provide all the important nutrients but potassium is often not included in sufficient quantities for the plants. This deficiency can be alleviated by adding bark compost from the gardening trade.

Mineral compound fertilizers, in contrast to organic fertilizers, are immediately at the disposal of the plants. Do not add these to the soil before the beginning of the growth period in mid spring. Follow the dosages recommended on the packaging. Also take account of the nutrient content of the soil (see p. 18) so that the herbaceous plants are not overloaded with nutrients. Because they work relatively quickly, mineral fertilizers are excellent for alleviating deficiencies.

Rules of fertilizing

- Do not use organic fertilizer before the first month of spring, nor mineral fertilizer before the second month of spring, otherwise the nutrients will be washed out of the soil by rainfall before they can be absorbed by your herbaceous plants.
- Do not give fertilizer after the first month of autumn. To do this would cause herbaceous plants to start another spurt of growth, and growing plants are particularly vulnerable to early frosts in autumn.
- Target the root area with the fertilizer. Carefully work the fertilizer into the soil with a rake.

NB: In the case of flat-rooting herbaceous plants like sunflower (*Helianthus*), mix the fertilizer with some soil and use a trowel to distribute the mixture around the plants to avoid damaging the roots.

- Overcast, rainy days are ideal for spreading fertilizer as the nutrients will be washed straight into the soil by the rain and any granules that may have accidentally landed on leaves are washed off very quickly. The granules could otherwise cause burn marks on leaves if the sun shines on them.

Symptoms of nutrient deficieny

If your herbaceous plants display any of the following symptoms, they may be suffering from nutrient deficiency, which requires immediate action:

- yellowish discoloration of the entire plant with many yellow leaves;
- early flowers at a completely atypical flowering time;
- meagre growth with weak stems;
- flowers that are too small, or very few flowers.

In such cases, fertilize with a quick-action liquid fertilizer or mineral compound fertilizer in a targeted fashion.

Caring for herbaceous plants

If you watch your herbaceous plants carefully and take action quickly when you spot problems such as dryness or growth of weeds, they will grow well and flower more prolifically.

Rules of watering

● During the first year, water as soon as there are any signs of dryness. This will help the roots to grow downwards quickly so that they can obtain nourishment from the deeper layers of the soil.

● From the second year onward do not water until the plants begin to look wilted.

● Always water long enough for the soil to be soaked to about a finger's length deep.

● Water in the mornings or evenings. The water will evaporate far less quickly or not at all and drops of water that have accidentally landed on leaves will not cause burns.

● Target water to individual herbaceous plants. If you water the spaces between plants, you will only encourage the growth of weeds.

● The finer the holes in the sprinkler, the more water will evaporate. Use a normal watering can or a garden hose with a sprinkler attachment.

● Cover the soil with a mulch layer so that it remains evenly moist.

● In cases of extreme drought, carefully hoe the surface of the soil so that the water can penetrate the soil more easily.

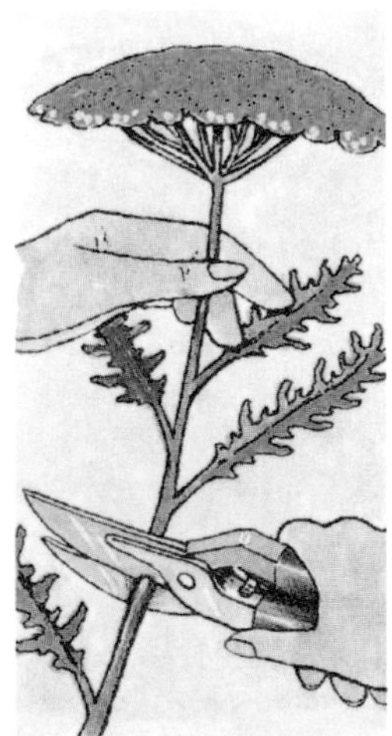

1 *The leafy stems of clumps can be cut off below the third leaf.*

2 *Leafless flower stems can be snipped off just above the ground.*

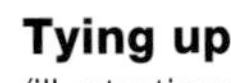

Tying up

(illustrations 4 and 5)

Tie up taller herbaceous plants carefully to prevent them from falling over. Use bought supports or thick hazel twigs for clumps and support canes for single shoots. Drive the support into the soil immediately after the plant has begun to shoot so that it will be disguised by the leaves.

Bought supports: Plastic supports soon become brittle and break. Metal supports covered in plastic are more durable. Drive them in all around a clump and tie the strings around the outside (see illustration 4).

Branches: Well-branching hazel twigs are cheaper. Push them in densely around the cluster, bend the tops over at different heights and weave them together (see illustration 5).

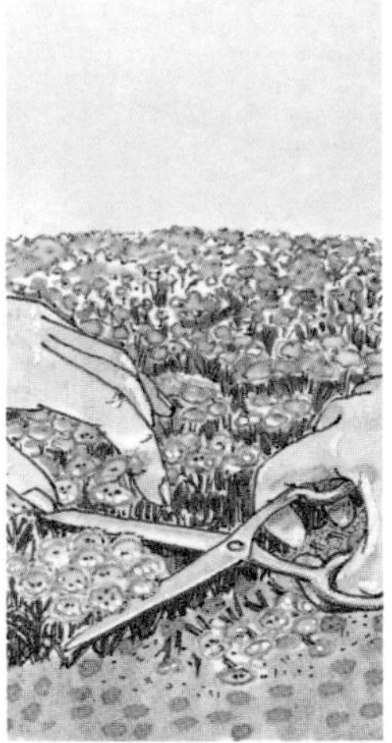

3 *Cushion plants can be shortened by half with kitchen scissors.*

4 Clumps can be tied up with sticks and twine.

Support posts: Long, weak individual shoots can be tied to a post or cane with garden twine.

Cutting back

(illustrations 1 and 3)

To keep a healthy bed and prevent plants from using up energy on producing seed, remove dead flowers during the growth period. In the winter, however, seedheads will provide an attractive picture. Do not cut down autumn-flowering plants until the following spring.

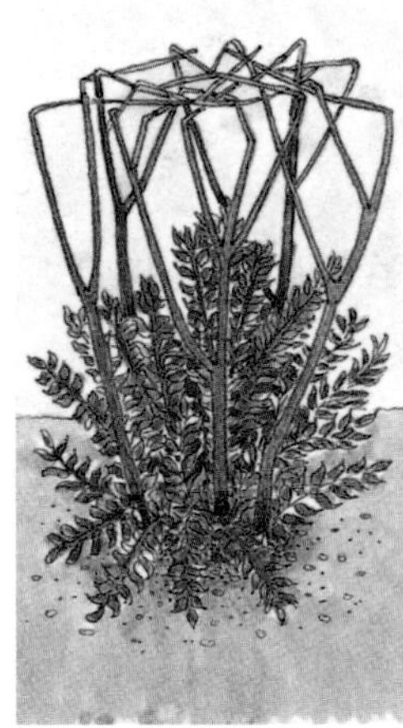

5 Clumps can be supported with hazel twigs,

Spring- and early-summer-flowering plants should be cut back immediately after flowering.

- In the case of clumps, cut off only the flower stalks below the third or fourth leaf as the leaves can remain standing (see illustration 1). Leafless flower stalks should be cut off close to the ground (see illustration 2).
- Cut back cushion plants by half. This will encourage them to produce new shoots and become bushy again the following year (see illustration 3).

Summer-flowering plants will often flower longer after the removal of dead flowers. Only cut off the very topmost tips as the lateral shoots often carry new flowerbuds.
Autumn-flowering plants and grasses should be cut back in early spring. Remove all dead shoots directly above the ground.
In the case of periwinkle, remove only the flower stalks.
Some herbaceous plants flower in early summer and then produce ***a second crop*** of flowers in late summer. To encourage such a second flowering, cut off the flower stalks immediately after the first flowering, directly above the ground, fertilize the plants and water well. This group includes *Delphinium, Leucanthemum*, catmint (*Nepeta*) and sage (*Salvia*).

Controlling weeds

Weeds will grow wherever there is room. Carefully remove the entire weed and use a trowel to remove the roots from the soil.
My tip: A cover of bark mulch is excellent for preventing weeds.

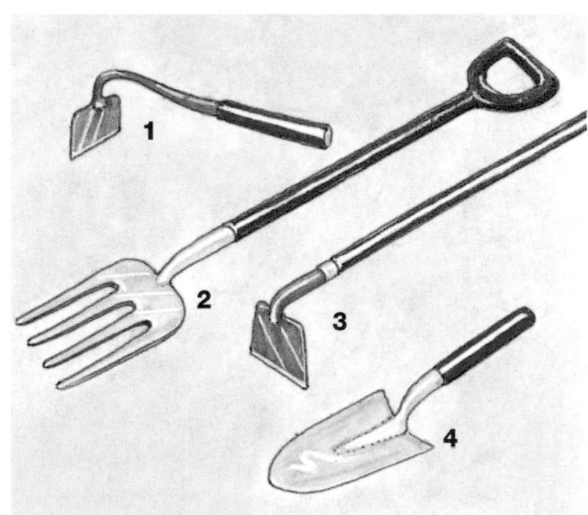

6 Garden tools: 1 Hand hoe for weeding; 2 Fork for loosening the soil; 3 Long hoe for weeding; 4 Trowel for planting.

Overwintering herbaceous plants

As the growing year comes to an end, it is time to carry out a thorough tidy up in the herbaceous bed. Winter is a difficult time for many plants as some are sensitive to frosts or risk decay in wet or damp weather. As a rule, however, winter protection is not necessary for a herbaceous border.
Herbaceous plants that have been planted in the autumn will require winter protection; also herbaceous plants that are sensitive to frost or decay, such as the alpine and Mediterranean plants (see p. 6). This group includes white rock cress (*Arabis caucasica*), thrift (*Armeria maritima*), campanula (*Campanula carpartica*, *C. glomerata*), *Centaurea macropetala*, *Crambe cordifolia*), globe thistle (*Echinops ritro*), sea holly (*Eryngium alpinum*), spurge (*Euphorbia* species), gypsophila (*Gypsophila paniculata*) and iris (*Iris barbata* hybrids). Protect these herbaceous plants with a layer of brushwood with perhaps a layer of dry leaves underneath.
My tip: Instead of brushwood you can also use a 10-20 cm (4-8 in) layer of compost over the herbaceous plant bed. You will be supplying nutrients to the plants, retaining a good soil structure and also preventing the herbaceous plants from growing upwards. The layer will also give winter protection to plants that are sensitive to frost or decay.

Rejuvenating herbaceous plants

The life expectancy of herbaceous plants varies (see p. 11). Many herbaceous plants begin to lose their vitality as the years go by and then will not flower much any more. Now is the time to take action and rejuvenate them by dividing them.
Method
- In the spring, dig out the herbaceous plant with a garden fork.
- Divide it into smaller pieces with a spade or knife but try to make sure that as few roots as possible are damaged by the process.
- After that, carefully untangle the roots with your hands.
- Each piece should have a fist-sized rootstock and at least three shoots.
- Discard the plant parts with meagre shoots on your compost heap.
- Replant the remaining parts (see p. 46).

NB: Long-lived herbaceous plants (see p. 11) require two to three years to become acclimatized. During this period they may sometimes look a little sickly. Give them time to grow and do not rejuvenate them again too soon.
My tip: Michaelmas daisies (*Aster novi-belgii, A. novi-angliae*) can be rejuvenated when they begin to look bare in the centre (see p. 10).

Thinning out dense groups

Even if you kept to the correct spacing when planting (see p. 46), a particular group of plants may become too dense after a few years. During the course of several years individual clumps may also become too thick.
You should start thinning out as soon as the following symptoms appear:
- The plants look sickly and produce only a few blooms.
- Herbaceous plants that always grew vigorously in the past do not seem to be doing so well.
- The plants are infested with downy mildew and grey mould (see p. 54).

If these symptoms are only found in one group or clump of plants, it will be sufficient for you just to give it plenty of fertilizer. If several plants in the same bed display the symptoms, you should thin out the entire stock.
Thinning out individual clumps: Take out single shoots close to the ground during the vegetation period. The remaining shoots should stand in a loose, airy

The first hoar frost casts its winter spell over the garden.

formation so that a light breeze could blow through the clump. In the spring you can divide the plant (see p. 52) so that it can continue to grow and flower.

Thinning out entire beds: If the herbaceous plants are all packed together too densely, take out individual plants. Remove different species to retain variety in the bed. If you dig out the plants carefully and divide them, you can plant the spare pieces somewhere else.

Crane's bill leaves covered in rime.

Pests and diseases

Plant protection begins when you are buying your plants in a nursery. Make sure that you purchase only healthy, strong plants in the first place (see p. 44).
It is also important to consider the requirements of herbaceous plants with respect to position, light, etc. when planning your garden (see p. 12). Also make sure that the soil contains a balanced nutrient content (see p. 18) and do not use special nitrogen fertilizers. A high nitrogen content will encourage growth but the plant tissues will become susceptible to fungal diseases. If you watch your herbaceous plants carefully, you will be able to thin out your stock in good time (see p. 52). Even a gentle breeze blowing through the plants can prevent pests from invading them. You will also be able to take action at the first sign of disease.

Choosing suitable neighbouring plants

Some plants actually ward off certain pests – for example, by their smell. Plant such helpful neighbours next to herbaceous plants that are frequently attacked by pests. Aphids often infest monkshood (*Aconitum*) and *Chrysanthmum maximum*. Lavender will help. Garlic (*Allium*)

The five most common diseases

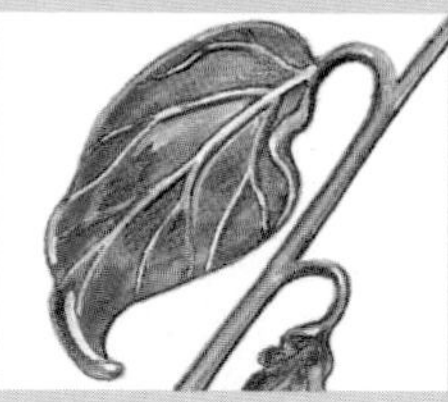

Grey mould
Symptoms: Young shoots and flowers wilt and decay and are covered in a film of greyish mould. ***Cause:*** High humidity; too much nitrogen.
Remedy: Remove infested shoots, thin out plants (see p. 52).

***Septoria* leaf spot disease**
Symptoms: A fungus causes round, dark spots on the leaves. The leaves turn brown if the infestation is severe.
Cause: High humidity.
Remedy: Remove infested leaves, also stalks of peonies.

Powdery mildew
Symptoms: Whitish, mealy film on leaves, shoots and flowers.
Cause: Dryness, heat; too much nitrogen. ***Remedy:*** Remove infested parts of plant; spray with mare's tail brew (see p. 56).

Downy mildew
Symptoms: A whitish fungal film on the undersides of the leaves, the leaves dry up. ***Cause:*** High humidity; stagnant air.
Remedy: Remove infested parts of the plant; thin out plants (see p. 52).

Rust
Symptoms: Orange red pustules on the undersides of leaves; yellow patches on the uppersides.
Cause: Damp, warm weather; nutrient deficiency. ***Remedy:*** Remove infested leaves; spray with tansy brew (see p. 56).

will drive away mites that infest autumn chrysanthemums (*Dendranthema indicum* hybrids). *Tagetes* is effective in combating eelworms, which often infest phlox. Herbaceous plants with fleshy roots, like peony (*Paeonia*), should be planted with *Narcissus* or garlic (*Allium*) as a preventive against voles.

Encouraging useful creatures

Useful creatures, the natural enemies of harmful organisms, will prevent masses of them from infesting your plants. Such useful predators will probably appear automatically but you can also encourage them in various ways. Useful insects often prefer certain plants. Hoverflies, for example, which consume large quantities of aphids, prefer parsley. Try to retain a large variety of plants in order to lure as many useful insect as possible into your garden. Small heaps of dead leaves or brushwood and other natural niches will serve as shelter for useful visitors such as ladybirds and hedgehogs.

The five most common pests

Nematodes (eelworms)
Symptoms: Crippled shoots and leaves; meagre growth.
Cause: Infestation. Nematodes can survive in the soil for many years.
Remedy: Remove infested plants. Leave these spots bare for some years.

Cuckoo spit
Symptoms: Crippled shoot tips and flowerbuds; from the middle of spring onwards foam clusters on flower stalks. ***Cause:*** Encouraged by long periods of drought. ***Remedy:*** Wash off both foam and the insect inside.

Aphids
Symptoms: Aphids on leaves; rolled up, crinkled leaves; sticky film.
Cause: Dryness; too much nitrogen.
Remedy: Remove severely infested shoots; spray with nettle brew or fermented herbal brew (see p. 56).

Slugs and snails
Symptoms: Holes eaten in leaves; slime trails. ***Cause:*** Moist, warm soil; mild winter. ***Remedy:*** Collect them; put down beer traps. Conifer needles and coarse gravel strewn around plants will deter them (see p. 56).

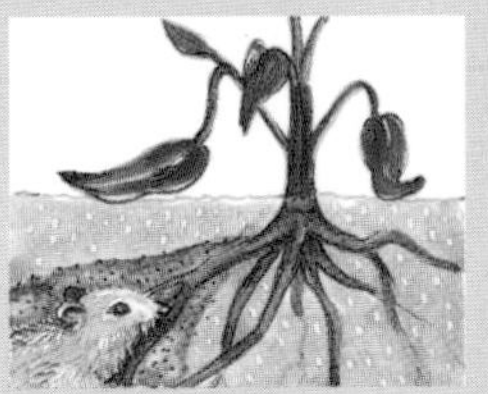

Voles
Symptoms: Wilting shoots and leaves; nibbled places on the roots.
Cause: Gnawing by voles.
Remedy: Humane traps. Release them in the wild. Plant narcissus and wild garlic.

Severe infestation

As soon as you discover the first symptoms of pests or disease in your herbaceous plants, you should ensure that the plants have optimal conditions for growth.

Light infestation: If the symptoms of disease are mild, give your herbaceous plants a good layer of compost and sufficient water and loosen the soil.

Fortify the plants' own resistance with herbal washes and fermented brews. These will also encourage the development of beneficial soil organisms. Washes are extracts of herbs made in a similar way to teas. Fermented brews are prepared like washes but then allowed to ferment. The herbal extracts will help to prevent certain pests from infesting the plants.

- Mare's tail brew (*Equisetum arvense*) for powdery mildew.
- Nettles (*Urtica dioica*) for aphids and spider mites.
- *Dryopteris* for scale insects, mealy bugs, red spider mites and rust.
- Tansy (*Chrysanthemum (Tanacetum) vulgare*) for aphids, white fly, rust and mildew.
- Garlic, onions and chives (*Allium*) for bacteria, mites and grey mould.

Spray the agents in overcast weather with a watering can or plant sprayer.

My tip: Herbal washes and fermented brews will keep in a cool cellar for one to two weeks. It is better to produce small amounts frequently rather than storing large quantities for too long.

Severe infestation: If your herbaceous plants have been severely infested, cut off the diseased parts of the plants and discard them in your refuse bin. Thin out the entire bed (see p. 52). Do not use chemical agents as they can kill many useful insects.

Recipes for washes and fermented brews

Use washes and fermented brews as a preventive every three to four weeks, reducing this to every ten days whenever there are symptoms of disease. 100 litres (22 gal) will be sufficient for an area of about 20-30 sq m (24-36 sq yd).

100 litres (22 gal) herbal wash: 1 kg (2 lb) fresh, chopped herbs or 150 g (about 6 oz) dried herbs are left to steep in 10 litres (17 pt) of water for 24 hours. Boil up for about half an hour and, after cooling, strain out the plant matter. Dilute this brew 1:10 with water and use for spraying.

100 litres (22 gal) fermented brew: 500 g (1 lb) fresh, chopped herbs or 75 g (about 3 oz) dried herbs added to 5 litres (9 pt) water in a vessel made of wood or plastic (not of metal!). Cover the vessel with a grid which will allow air to circulate, and stir once or twice daily. After twelve days, fermentation should have ceased. Strain the extract and mix with water in the ratio of 1:20, then spray.

Control of slugs and snails

Slugs can become a veritable plague in a herbaceous border in moist, warm weather. You can try the following measures in the case of slug or snail infestation.

- In the evenings, lay damp wooden planks on the soil and collect the creatures from underneath them in the mornings.
- Slug bait or a beer trap may work. NB: Do not use these if you have small children or domestic pets.
- Strew grit, wood shavings, sawdust or conifer needles around the herbaceous plants at risk.

If none of these measures alleviates the problem, you may have to use slug pellets. As they are very toxic, you should keep strictly to the instructions on the packaging. During the weeks after strewing them, neither children nor domestic pets should be allowed in the garden. Collect dead slugs, as poisoned slugs will kill birds.

Healthy herbaceous plants will bloom year after year.

Index

Numbers in **bold** indicate illustrations.

Author's notes

This volume deals with the planting and care of herbaceous plants. Lethally toxic plants or even less toxic ones, some of which may cause considerable damage to health, are marked with a warning symbol in the tables on pages 16 and 17. Make absolutely sure that children and domestic pets are not able to eat plants or parts of plants marked in this way. When working with garden tools or soil, you may incur injuries. In both cases, consult your physician and discuss the possibility of having a vaccination against tetanus.
All fertilizers and plant protection agents, even the biological ones, should be stored in such a way that they are inaccessible to children and domestic pets. Consumption of these agents may lead to damage to health. They should not be allowed to come into contact with your eyes. Take note of all safety precautions provided on packaging, particularly in the case of slug pellets (see p. 56).

Photographic acknowledgements
Jürgen Becker: inside front cover, p. 2, 5 right, 8 right, 9 top left, top right, 18 top, 24/25, 25 right, 32, 35 top, 47 bottom, 48, 53 top, bottom, 57, 62/3.
Marion Nickig: front cover, 3 left, right, 4/5, 7, 8 left, 9 centre right, bottom left, bottom right, 12, 14 left, right, 15 (all photos), 18 bottom, 22 top, bottom, 28, 34 (all photos), 35 bottom left, bottom right, 37, 38, 40, 42/43, 43 right, 45, 47 top, back cover.

Acknowledgements
Both the photographers and the publishers would like to thank the following garden owners and designers for their kind permission to take photographs:
Arends, Wuppertal: p. 47; Bennekom, Domburg (Netherlands): p. 24/25, 35 top; Greve, Heerlon (Netherlands): p. 18 top, 45; Jonker, Sybekarpsel (Netherlands): Inside front cover; Stuurmann, Bergen (Netherlands): p. 2, 48; Suhrborg, Wesel: p. 8 right; Ter Linden, Ruinen (Netherlands): p. 32, 57; Van Steeg, Dinxperloo (Netherlands): p. 53 top.

Cover photographs
Front cover: *The red flowers of lupins make a wonderful contrast with the blue of the delphiniums.*
Inside front cover: *A colour run in shades of red, pink, and lilac, lightened with white blooms.*
Back cover: *An autumnal mood in the herbaceous border with stonecrop, red hot pokers and autumn asters.*

This edition published 1997 by
Merehurst Limited
Ferry House, 51-57 Lacy Road,
Putney, London SW15 1PR

ISBN 1 85391 637 4

A catalogue record for this book is available from the British Library.

Translated by Astrid Mick
Edited by Lesley Young
Design and typesetting by
Paul Cooper Design
Printed in Hong Kong by
Wing King Tong

The splendour of winter

As the gardening year draws to a close the cheerful display of colour gradually disappears from herbaceous beds. Soft shades of brown dominate in the garden and allow the interesting shapes of the last flowers and grasses to stand out. When hoar frost covers the plants like a layer of sugar, a magical scene is created. Do not cut back these autumn-flowering plants until the spring so that they can continue to provide interest during the autumn and winter.

The flowers and seedheads of stonecrop and grasses remain decorative even in winter.

Other titles available in the series